Contents

Acknowledgments

COI gratefully acknowledges the help of the Ministry of Agriculture, Fisheries and Food, the Scottish Office Agriculture and Fisheries Department, the Welsh Office, the Department of Agriculture for Northern Ireland, the Agricultural and Food Research Council and the Forestry Commission in the preparation of this book.

Thanks are also due to the National Sheep Association, the Rural Development Commission, the Scottish Office Information Department, *New Farmer and Grower*, the Wales Tourist Board and HRI for special help with the photographs.

Photograph Credits

Numbers refer to the pages in the illustration section (1–8):

Institute of Agricultural History, University of Reading, p. 2 (top and centre); Communications Unit, Department of Agriculture for Northern Ireland, pp. 2 (bottom), 4 (top), 5 (top); Wales Tourist Board, p. 3 (bottom); *Farmers' Weekly* (photos by Raymond Lea), pp. 3 (centre), 5 (centre); HRI, p. 4 (bottom); Scottish Office Agriculture and Fisheries Department, p. 3 (top); *New Farmer and Grower* magazine, p. 4 (centre); National Sheep Association, p. 5 (bottom); Highlands and Islands Enterprise, p. 6 (top); Rural Development Commission, p. 6 (centre); Forestry Commission, p. 6 (bottom); Mr W.H.M. Lewis, p. 7 (bottom); Peterhead Corporation, p. 7 (top); COI, p. 8 (top); AFRC Institute of Food Research, p. 8 (bottom).

The cover photograph, of a farm near Patterdale (Cumbria), is by courtesy of the National Sheep Association.

Agriculture, Fisheries
and Forestry

London: H M S O

Researched and written by Reference Services,
Central Office of Information.

This book is an expanded version, including much historical
material, of the chapter on Agriculture, Fisheries and Forestry in
Britain 1993: An Official Handbook.

ISBN 0 11 701724 8

HMSO publications are available from:

HMSO Publications Centre
(Mail, fax and telephone orders only)
PO Box 276, London SW8 5DT
Telephone orders 071-873 9090
General enquiries 071-873 0011
(queuing system in operation for both numbers)
Fax orders 071-873 8200

HMSO Bookshops
49 High Holborn, London WC1V 6HB   071-873 0011
Fax 071-873 8200 (counter service only)
258 Broad Street, Birmingham B1 2HE   021-643 3740   Fax 021-643 6510
Southey House, 33 Wine Street, Bristol BS1 2BQ
0272 264306   Fax 0272 294515
9-21 Princess Street, Manchester M60 8AS   061-834 7201   Fax 061-833 0634
16 Arthur Street, Belfast BT1 4GD   0232 238451   Fax 0232 235401
71 Lothian Road, Edinburgh EH3 9AZ   031-228 4181   Fax 031-229 2734

HMSO's Accredited Agents
(see Yellow Pages)

and through good booksellers

Introduction:
Agriculture Today

British agriculture is noted for its high level of efficiency and productivity. In 1991 it employed 2.1 per cent of the total workforce and Britain[1] was self-sufficient in 58 per cent of all types of food and animal feed. It was self-sufficient in nearly 74 per cent of indigenous-type food and feed. Food, feed and beverages accounted for over 10 per cent of Britain's imports by value in 1991, compared with about a quarter in the 1960s. The agricultural contribution to gross domestic product (GDP) was £6,324 million in 1991, about 1.3 per cent of the total. Britain is also a major exporter of agricultural produce and food products, agrochemicals and agricultural machinery.

The Government aims to foster an efficient and competitive agricultural industry through the provision and sponsorship of research, development and advisory services; the provision of financial support where appropriate; measures to control disease, pests and pollution; and improved marketing arrangements for food and food products. It also insists on high standards of animal welfare. Agriculture ministers must balance the needs of an efficient agricultural industry with other interests in the countryside. These include conservation of its natural beauty and promotion of its enjoyment by the public.

---

[1]'Britain' is used informally in this book to mean the United Kingdom of Great Britain and Northern Ireland. 'Great Britain' comprises England, Scotland and Wales.

Land Use

The area of agricultural land has been declining, although there has been a reduction in the net rate of loss in recent years. In 1991 there were just under 11.9 million hectares (29.3 million acres) under crops and grass. Some 5.9 million hectares (14.6 million acres) were used for rough grazing, most of it in hilly areas. Soils vary from the thin poor ones of highland Britain to the rich fertile soils of low-lying areas such as the fenlands of eastern England. The temperate climate and the relatively even distribution of rainfall over the year ensure a long growing season; streams rarely dry up and grassland normally remains green throughout the year.

Land Use in Britain

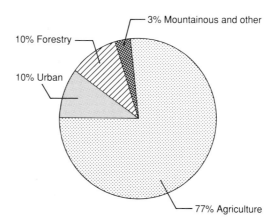

3% Mountainous and other

10% Forestry

10% Urban

77% Agriculture

Farming

In 1991 there were some 241,000 farm holdings in Britain (excluding minor holdings), with an average size of 71 hectares (175 acres)—again excluding minor holdings. About two-thirds of all agricultural land is owner-occupied. About 40 per cent of holdings are of 4 British Standard Units (BSUs)[2] or less.

The number of people (excluding spouses) engaged in agriculture in 1991 was about 552,000, compared with 565,000 in 1990 and an average of 639,000 in 1980–82. The total for whole-time farmers, partners and directors in 1991—about 178,300—had declined from 183,500 in 1990 and from an average of 206,000 in 1980–82. The number of farmers, partners and directors working part-time—100,400 in 1991—has continued to increase (from an average of 89,000 in 1980–82 and of 98,100 in 1990). Regular whole-time workers (family and hired) have continued to decline—to 119,500 in 1991—compared with 125,200 in 1990 and an average of 174,000 in 1980–82. The number of regular part-time workers (family and hired) remained at about the same level as in 1990, at some 58,700, compared with an average of 63,000 in 1980–82.

Labour productivity has increased by 51 per cent over the last ten years. Total income from farming (that of farmers, partners, directors and their spouses) was £2,168 million in 1991, 6 per cent less than in 1990.

At the end of 1990 the industry's capital stock amounted to some £23,710 million (compared with £24,000 million at the end of 1989), of which buildings and works made up nearly two-thirds. The overall stock of fixed capital is estimated to be at a similar level to the average for 1980–82.

In 1991 there were over 400,000 tractors and over 40,000 combine harvesters in use. Most farms have a direct electricity supply,

---

[2]BSUs measure the financial potential of the holding in terms of the margins which might be expected from its crops and stock.

Agricultural Land Use 1991

TOTAL AREA ON AGRICULTURAL
HOLDINGS

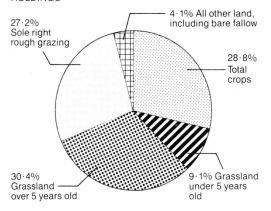

27·2%
Sole right
rough grazing

4·1% All other land,
including bare fallow

28·8%
Total
crops

30·4%
Grassland
over 5 years old

9·1% Grassland
under 5 years
old

CROPS

4·0% Horticulture

10·9% Other crops

4·1%
Peas and
beans

3·9%
Sugar
beet

8·9%
Oilseed
rape

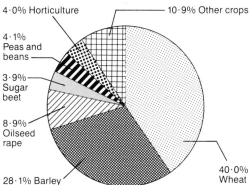

28·1% Barley

40·0%
Wheat

the remainder having their own generators. Horticultural crops such as blackcurrants and brussels sprouts are frequently harvested by machine, and milking machines are used on the vast majority of dairy farms.

Most farms in Britain produce a range of commodities. In choosing both their products and their inputs, farmers may be assisted by computer models.

Further information on developments in agriculture, fisheries and forestry is contained in *Current Affairs: A Monthly Survey*, published by HMSO.

Historical Background

England

Early English agriculture was largely based on the open-field system, but common ownership and collective cultivation of open fields were seen as a barrier to progress, even though the system allowed for permanent arable rotation: winter corn; spring corn; fallow.

The Black Death of the mid-fourteenth century deepened the recession in English agriculture. Recovery started in the fifteenth century, and England became famous for its sheep, both for mutton and for the profits to be gained from the wool trade. Open fields began to be enclosed for grazing land, holdings were enlarged and consolidated, and arable land was lost to grazing. It has been estimated that some 2.43 million hectares (6 million acres) of English fields were enclosed between 1700 and 1845.

In the seventeenth century potatoes, red clover and turnips were introduced, and these crops made feeding large flocks of sheep during the winter much easier. The four-course rotation system was established in Norfolk during the century. Its essential feature was the alternation of a straw crop with a root or seeds crop. This meant wheat in the first year, roots (turnips or swedes) in the second, barley with ryegrass and clover in the third, and the clover and ryegrass either grazed or cut for feed in the fourth. The system gave greater fertility, heavier cereal yields and abundant animal feed, and by 1800 it was general in England and was being used in Scotland. By the mid-nineteenth century it had been adopted in much of continental Europe. It has been considerably varied, but remains the foundation of modern husbandry.

Jethro Tull (1674–1741), of Prosperous Farm, Shalbourne (Wiltshire), pioneered the horse-drawn hoe and the mechanical seed drill. Corn could then grow efficiently in rows, leaving room for turnips and other root crops. Charles Viscount Townshend (1674–1738), nicknamed 'Turnip', and Thomas Coke (1752–1842; later 1st Earl of Leicester) were pioneers in the development of crop husbandry; their research in establishing new crops made it easier to carry livestock and laid the basis of sound crop rotation. The latter spent half a million pounds on his estate and raised his annual rents from £2,000 to £20,000. Of those who worked to improve the quality of their cattle and sheep, Robert Bakewell (1725–95), of Dishley in Leicestershire, who vastly improved the quality of his Leicester sheep through rigid selection and culling, achieved most fame. Many breeds were improved or established on Bakewell's lines. Breed societies were set up from the late eighteenth century to maintain standards.

Among significant foundations in England may be mentioned those of the Bath and West of England Agricultural Society in 1777; the Board of Agriculture (precursor of the Ministry of Agriculture, Fisheries and Food) in 1793; the Smithfield Club in 1798; the Royal Agricultural Society of England in 1838; and the Royal Agricultural College, Cirencester (Gloucestershire) in 1845.

Wales

Radical changes in Welsh agriculture, hitherto at subsistence level, began as a result of the plague outbreaks of the fourteenth century; the political stability which followed the union with England in 1535; and the division of the border country into shires. Plague and

a high death rate caused a land surplus, which encouraged enclosure of open arable fields, creating compact farms. Political stability opened up more distant markets and assisted in the consolidation
of estates and the enclosure of wasteland and commons.

By the second half of the sixteenth century, a more commercial system of agriculture meant that produce began to be marketed
in distant, expanding cities, such as London. The most common
crops were wheat and oats, although barley was also widely grown.
Liming enabled fairly intensive working, and productivity in the
lowland areas appears to have been high by the standards of the
day. As well as grain, butter and cheese were marketed, but by far
the most important exports were the products of pastoral farming:
store cattle (eight to ten months old), wool and cloth. Sheep were
also driven on the hoof to markets in England, but it was more
usual for wool to be sold in Wales.

Though commercial farming had brought many benefits to
Welsh farms, agricultural innovation lagged well behind that in
most of England and especially behind the farming methods in the
major arable areas. The main lowland markets were distant, the
road network was poor, and the emphasis was on pastoral farming.
Even so, the Brecknockshire Agricultural Society, founded in 1755,
was one of the earliest agricultural societies in the British Isles.
Great landowners, prime movers in agricultural reform in
England, were rare in Wales, while smaller owners lacked the capital to institute widespread change.

The demand for grain during the Napoleonic Wars gave farmers greater incentive to increase food output; as much land as possible was ploughed and production methods were improved. New
techniques from England now began to be adopted in Wales, especially in the lowlands, where the larger, richer landowners benefited

the most. There were efforts to modernise means of transport and the enclosure of wasteland and commons accelerated. Over 80,000 hectares (200,000 acres) were enclosed between 1793 and 1815.

The Glamorgan Agricultural Society was founded in 1772, that of Cardiganshire (Dyfed) in 1784, and by 1815 there were local or county societies in all parts of Wales. They played an important role in the improvement of grassland and the introduction of crop rotation.

Scotland

The Honourable Society of Improvers, founded in 1723, included peers, lawyers, landlords and academics, all interested in the new agricultural ideas from England. Enclosures were as unpopular among the Scottish peasantry as they were in England. New ideas had greatest success in the Lothians and Aberdeenshire. Cultivation of the potato, first planted in Scotland in the late 1730s, spread rapidly. The average weight of cattle doubled during the century; Berwickshire and the Lothians raised rich grain crops; Ayrshire became famous for dairy farming; Galloway for stock-breeding; and the Borders for sheep.

From the 1760s huge sheep farms in the Highlands brought unemployment and hastened emigration, but by the 1820s the wool market at Inverness had become famous.

During the nineteenth century, tenants in the Highlands and Islands, on land which their ancestors had farmed for centuries, but who used old methods and could not pay increased rents, were forcibly evicted to make way for sheep farms. These Clearances were stopped by the Crofters Act 1886.

Scottish oats, potatoes, turnips and barley provided reliable crops. The fame of Aberdeen Angus and Ayrshire cattle, and of border sheep, spread wider.

Credit for the invention of the world's first useful threshing machine (1786) is given to the Scot Andrew Meikle (1719–1811). Another Scot, Patrick Bell (1799–1869), built the first successful mechanised reaper in 1826.

Among significant foundations in Scotland were the Highland and Agricultural Society of Scotland in 1784 and the Chair of Agriculture and Rural Economy at Edinburgh University in 1790.

Northern Ireland

The English and Scottish immigrants of the early seventeenth century found large forests, rivers teeming with fish, and fertile arable land, and the Irish engaged in a pastoral economy with cattle the basic means of support. There were no enclosed fields and ploughing was inefficient; land was shared out, with no one permanently owning any part of it. There were no towns and no significant villages.

Many of the newcomers were of modest means and became working farmers and not distant landlords. 'Good tillage and husbandry after the English manner' meant better tools, techniques and livestock breeds, although the Scots were noted as enthusiastic tillers, and producers of oats and barley. This helps to explain why the Irish Land Acts of the late nineteenth century, which enabled peasant farmers to obtain loans to buy their holdings from the landlord, did not have so radical an effect in Northern Ireland. In 1925 another Act enabled 40,000 farmers—virtually all of the remainder —to acquire their holdings. Almost all farmland in Northern Ireland is therefore owner-occupied.

By the mid-1920s farming employed about one-quarter of the labour force. This figure remained constant until 1945, when it represented some 180,000 people on about 90,000 farms—the largest industry in Northern Ireland. Northern Ireland was dotted with small family farms, about two-thirds of which were between 0.50 and 12 hectares (1.24 and 30 acres). This structure, together with soil and climate, has created an emphasis on livestock, especially beef cattle, dairy cows and sheep. There has been a decline in the number of farming units, to 33,000 in 1983 and to 29,000 in 1991. This process of amalgamation means that farms now have an average area of almost 35 hectares (86 acres)—more than twice the average for the European Community, but still below average farm size in Britain.

Britain

At the end of the eighteenth century Britain, with a population of 10.7 million, was predominantly rural and largely self-sufficient in food. It has been estimated that by the mid-nineteenth century British agriculture provided nearly 95 per cent of the calories needed by the population of Britain. In 1851 agriculture was still Britain's largest industry, holding its own against the new industries of the industrial revolution and employing 1.79 million people.

From the 1870s strong overseas competition led to a marked rise in imports of wheat, meat, dairy produce, fruit and feed. Prices fell and the number of agricultural labourers continued to drop, while the area of land under cultivation fell by over 30 per cent between 1871 and 1901.

In 1843 the world's first agricultural experimental station opened at Rothamsted (Hertfordshire). Here were laid the foundations of today's worldwide artificial fertiliser practice and the importance of soil micro-organisms was first emphasised; the possibilities of soil sterilisation first exploited; and the extraction of protein from leaf material pioneered. Sir John Bennet Lawes

(1814–1900), to whom Rothamsted belonged, and Sir Joseph Gilbert (1817–1901) introduced scientifically proven methods of farming—Lawes establishing that nitrogen, potassium and phosphorus are the elements most needed as chemical fertilisers.

Unlike most other European countries, Britain had few restraints on imports of agricultural produce and in the early twentieth century it had become the world's foremost food importer: by 1909-13 it was importing 79 per cent of its grain needs, 40 per cent of its meat, 72 per cent of its dairy produce, 73 per cent of its fruit and 62 per cent of its feed. Between 1914 and 1927 the area of ploughland in England and Wales declined by some 300,000 hectares (741,000 acres).

The need to promote home production in the 1920s, and the world depression in the early 1930s, however, caused governments to give some protection to farmers. By the Agricultural Credits Act 1923, agricultural credit societies were organised to advance loans to members for approved agricultural purposes. By the Agricultural Credits Act 1928, loans could be secured on farming stock and other assets, through a company created for the purpose. Its resources were increased in 1939. The Agricultural Marketing Acts 1931 and 1933 enabled producers to set up marketing boards to control the marketing of various commodities. With the outbreak of the second world war in 1939 maximum output, with stringent measures against any farmer who refused to co-operate, became official policy. Between 1938 and 1943 the index of gross agricultural production (measured in calories) rose by 55 per cent and imports of food and feed were reduced by as much as 85 per cent; the proportionate increase in net output was 91 per cent.

The Agriculture Act 1947 sought to provide stability through guaranteed prices and assured markets, and to encourage agricultural production amid the shortages after the second world war. From the mid-1950s worldwide food production greatly increased and the problem of surpluses arose. To discourage surpluses, standard production quantities were introduced for milk, eggs, potatoes, wheat and other goods, and price guarantees applied only to these quantities; if production went beyond them, the average price received by all producers was lowered.

Agriculture's share of GDP declined from 17 per cent in 1867–69 to 6 per cent in 1911–13 and (with forestry and fishing) 3 per cent in 1966–68 and 1.3 per cent in 1991. These figures reflect a decline in area cultivated, but also a much more intensive industry—in an extended production process—which has increasingly complex links with the economy.

Production

Home production of the principal foods is shown in Table 1 as a percentage by weight of total supplies (that is, production plus imports minus exports).[3]

Livestock

Over half of full-time farms are devoted mainly to dairying or beef cattle and sheep. The majority of sheep and cattle are reared in the hill and moorland areas of Scotland, Wales, Northern Ireland and northern and south-western England. Beef fattening occurs partly in better grassland areas, as does dairying, and partly on arable farms. British livestock breeders have developed many of the cattle, sheep and pig breeds with worldwide reputations, for example, the Hereford and Aberdeen Angus beef breeds, the Jersey, Guernsey and Ayrshire dairy breeds, Large White pigs and a number of sheep breeds. Because of developments in artificial insemination and embryo transfer, Britain is able to export semen and embryos from high-quality donor animals.

Cattle and Sheep

Most dairy cattle in Britain are bred by artificial insemination. In 1991 the average size of dairy herds in Britain was 63 (excluding minor holdings), while the average yield of milk per dairy cow was 5,143 litres (1,131 gallons). Average household consumption of liquid (including low-fat) milk per head in 1991 was 1.09 litres (1.91 pints) a week.

[3]Output equals production minus what is kept for use on farms or for farm stocks.

About two-thirds of home-fed beef production originates from the national dairy herd, in which the Friesian breed is predominant. The remainder is derived from suckler herds producing high-quality beef calves in the hills and uplands, where the traditional British beef breeds, such as Hereford and Aberdeen Angus, continue to be important. Imported breeds which have been established include the Charolais, Limousin, Simmental and Belgian Blue. In 1991 the average size of the beef-breeding herd continued to expand and reached its highest level for 14 years. This increase partially offset the further decrease in the dairy herd.

Table 1: British Production as a Percentage of Total New Supplies

Food product	1980–82 average	1991 (provisional)
Beef and veal	92	95
Eggs	100	95
Milk for human con- sumption (as liquid)	100	100
Cheese	70	67
Butter	59	60
Sugar (as refined)	51	61
Wheat	98	125
Potatoes	93	90

Source: Ministry of Agriculture, Fisheries and Food.

Britain has a long tradition of sheep production, with more than 40 breeds and many crosses between them. Research has provided vaccine and serum protection against nearly all the epidemic diseases. Although lamb production is the main source of income for sheep farmers, wool is also important.

Grass supplies 60 to 80 per cent of the feed for cattle and sheep. Grass production has been enhanced by the increased use of fertilisers, methods of grazing control and improved herbage conservation for winter feed. Rough grazings are used for extensively grazed sheep and cattle, producing young animals for fattening elsewhere.

Pigs and Poultry

Pig production occurs in most areas but is particularly important in eastern and northern England. There is an increasing concentration into specialist units and larger herds.

Output of poultrymeat has continued to benefit from better husbandry and genetic improvements. Production of broilers from holdings of over 100,000 birds accounts for over half of total production. In 1991 British egg production continued to recover following stringent government measures to deal with salmonella. Output of hen and duck eggs rose from 813 million dozen in 1990 to 841 million dozen in 1991. Over two-thirds of laying birds are on holdings with 20,000 or more birds. Britain remains broadly self-sufficient in poultrymeat and eggs.

Animal Welfare

The welfare of farm animals is protected by legislation and it is an offence to cause unnecessary pain or distress to commercially reared livestock. For example, there are regulations requiring owners of intensive units to arrange for the daily inspection of their stock and the equipment on which it depends. There is increased protection for all livestock, poultry, rabbits and horses at markets, and specific controls on the marketing of foals and calves. There are laws which ban close confinement crates for keeping veal calves and which will phase out tether and close confinement systems for keeping pigs, and protect animals at slaughter from unnecessary pain or distress. The Farm Animal Welfare Council, an independent body set up by the Government, advises on any legislative or other changes it considers necessary. Britain continues to take the lead in pressing for higher standards of animal welfare throughout Europe. The Government's proposed charter on animal welfare in the European Community aims to raise welfare standards.

Table 2: Livestock and Livestock Products

	1980–82 average	1989	1990	1991 (provisional)
Cattle and calves ('000 head)	13,269	11,975	12,059	11,866
Sheep and lambs ('000 head)	32,204	42,988	43,799	43,621
Pigs ('000 head)	7,889	7,509	7,449	7,596
Poultry ('000 head)[a]	80,400	89,246	92,341	94,605
Milk (million litres)	15,557	14,232	14,521	14,077
Eggs (million dozen)	1,127	848	891	922
Beef and veal ('000 tonnes)	1,039	972	998	1,021
Mutton and lamb ('000 tonnes)	280	385	393	418
Pork ('000 tonnes)	716	731	749	797
Bacon and ham ('000 tonnes)	202	194	180	175
Poultrymeat ('000 tonnes)	772	993	1,025	1,063

Source: Ministry of Agriculture, Fisheries and Food.
[a] Includes ducks, geese and turkeys. Figures for turkeys are for England and Wales only from 1986.

Crops

The farms devoted primarily to arable crops are found mainly in eastern and central-southern England and eastern Scotland. In Britain in 1991 cereals were grown on 3.52 million hectares (8.7 million acres), compared with 3.66 million hectares (9.04 million acres) in 1990. Production of cereals, at 22.7 million tonnes, was similar to that in 1990. An increase in plantings of higher-yielding wheat contributed to increased output—13.2 million tonnes, compared with 12.9 million tonnes in 1990.

Between 40 and 50 per cent of available domestic wheat supplies (allowing for imports and exports) are normally used for flour milling, and about half for animal feed. About one-third of barley supplies is used for malting and distilling, and virtually all the remainder for animal feed.

There was a significant increase in the area planted to oilseed rape—from 390,000 hectares (963,700 acres) in 1990 to an estimated 445,000 hectares (1.1 million acres) in 1991. Production was about 1.31 million tonnes, a small increase over 1990 production.

Large-scale potato and vegetable cultivation is undertaken in the fens (in Cambridgeshire and south Lincolnshire), the alluvial areas around the rivers Thames and Humber, and the peaty lands in south Lancashire. Early potatoes are an important crop in Pembrokeshire (Dyfed), Kent and Cornwall. High-grade seed potatoes are grown in Scotland and Northern Ireland. Production of peas in 1991 for harvesting dry (including those for human consumption) came to an estimated 262,000 tonnes; production of beans was 437,000 tonnes.

Sugar from home-grown sugar beet provides just over 60 per cent of requirements, most of the remainder being refined from raw cane sugar imported duty-free from developing countries under the Lomé Convention. White sugar production from beet is estimated at 1.27 million tonnes.

Table 3: Main Crops

	1980–82 average	1989	1990	1991 (provisional)
Wheat				
Area ('000 hectares)	1,532	2,083	2,013	1,990
Production ('000 tonnes)	9,163	14,033	14,033	14,333
Yield (tonnes per hectare)	5.98	6.74	6.97	7.20
Barley				
Area ('000 hectares)	2,294	1,653	1,517	1,401
Production ('000 tonnes)	10,502	8,073	7,897	7,707
Yield (tonnes per hectare)	4.58	4.88	5.21	5.50
Oats				
Area ('000 hectares)	140	119	107	105
Production ('000 tonnes)	598	529	530	545
Yield (tonnes per hectare)	4.27	4.46	4.96	5.18
Potatoes				
Area ('000 hectares)	197	175	178	177
Production ('000 tonnes)	6,693	6,262	6,480	6,354
Yield (tonnes per hectare)	33.97[a]	35.78	36.40	35.89
Oilseed rape				
Area ('000 hectares)	130	321	390	445
Production ('000 tonnes)	407	976	1,258	1,308
Yield (tonnes per hectare)	3.12	3.04	3.23	2.94
Sugar beet				
Area ('000 hectares)	209	197	194	196
Production ('000 tonnes)	8,261	8,113	7,902	7,900
Yield (tonnes per hectare)	39.57	41.28	40.66	40.32

Sources: Agriculture in the United Kingdom: 1991 and Agricultural Census
June 1991

[a]1982 figure only

Horticulture

In 1991 the land utilised for horticulture (excluding potatoes) was about 200,000 hectares (494,220 acres). Vegetables grown in the open accounted for 68 per cent of this, orchards for 17 per cent, soft fruit for 7 per cent and ornamentals (including hardy nursery stock, bulbs and flowers grown in the open) for 7 per cent. In some cases more than one vegetable crop is taken from the same area of land in a year, so that the estimated area actually cropped in 1991 was 259,400 hectares (641,000 acres).

Field vegetables account for about one-third of the value of horticultural output and are widely grown throughout the country. Most horticultural enterprises are increasing productivity with the help of improved planting material, new techniques and the widespread use of machinery. Some field vegetables, for example, are raised in blocks of compressed peat or loose-filled cells, a technique which reduces root damage and allows plants to establish themselves more reliably and evenly.

Glasshouses are used for growing tomatoes, cucumbers, sweet peppers, lettuces, flowers, pot plants and nursery stock. Widespread use is made of automatic control of heating and ventilation and semi-automatic control of watering. Energy-efficient glasshouses use thermal screens, while low-cost plastic tunnels extend the season for certain crops previously grown in the open. Government grants are available for replacing heated glass and heating systems.

The Government also provides grants for replanting apple and pear trees. Output of apples in Britain in 1991 was some 268,000 tonnes, compared with 270,000 tonnes in 1990.

Under the European Community's Common Agricultural Policy (see below), a wide range of horticultural produce is subject to common quality standards.

Under Community rules, Britain has a production limit of 2.5 million litres of wine a year; it is produced in southern England and South Wales. A pilot Quality Wine Scheme was launched by the Government for the 1991 vintage.

Organic Farming

The Government aims to establish a framework in which organic farming in Britain can respond to consumer demand. The organic sector is eligible for the support given to all farmers under a number of general schemes. Other support includes a significant commitment to research and development.

The United Kingdom Register of Organic Food Standards (UKROFS) is an independent body set up in 1987 with government support. It has established national voluntary standards for organic food production tied to a certification and inspection scheme. It is also responsible for enforcing the Community regulation on organic foodstuffs, adopted in June 1991, which sets production, processing and labelling standards for organic produce within the Community.

It is estimated that in 1991, 100,000 hectares (247,000 acres) were being farmed organically in Britain. Most organic farms specialise in horticulture, although significant numbers produce cereals, particularly in Scotland. Many Welsh organic farms specialise in livestock.

Food Safety

Government spending on programmes to promote food safety and against diseases affecting food supply is over £100 million in 1992–93. Its expenditure on food safety research will total £18.5 million. Recent investigations have covered the performance of microwave ovens and the handling of chilled food.

The Food Safety Directorate within the Ministry of Agriculture, Fisheries and Food focuses Ministry resources on ensuring adequate supplies of the right kinds of food, and its safety, wholesomeness and proper labelling, through regulations and guidelines. Food safety responsibilities are separated from food production and agriculture responsibilities within the Ministry. The Government's commitment to food safety was emphasised by the Food Safety Act 1990, which ensures food safety and consumer protection throughout the food chain. It combines basic provisions with wide enabling powers, so that detailed regulations made under the Act can adapt to technological change and innovation. It also introduces more effective enforcement powers and greatly increased penalties for offenders. A number of independent advisory committees consisting of recognised experts advise the Government on the exercise of powers under the Act.

—The Food Advisory Committee advises ministers on the exercise of powers relating to the labelling, composition and chemical safety of food.

—The Advisory Committee on Novel Foods and Processes advises on any matter relating to the irradiation of food or to the manufacture of novel foods or foods produced by novel processes.

—The Steering Group on the Chemical Aspects of Food Surveillance is charged with keeping under review possible chemical contamination of the national food supply and monitoring the intakes of food additives and nutrients. It is assisted by 11 working parties covering detailed aspects of its work.

—The Advisory Committee on the Microbiological Safety of Food advises on matters relating to this topic and there is also a Steering Group on the Microbiological Safety of Food.

—In addition, a consumer panel—nine consumer members nominated by the main consumer organisations, but appointed to serve as individuals—gives consumers a direct means of conveying their views on food safety and consumer protection issues to the Government.

National regulations to implement European Community measures have also been introduced. In 1991 these covered exports, packaging materials in contact with food, additives, fruit juices and animal feed.

Exports and Marketing

Today Britain imports about 42 per cent of its food. The Government encourages the growth of exports related to agriculture. The volume of these exports rose in 1991, when their value amounted to £5,792 million, the main markets being Western Europe, North America and the Middle East. Exports include speciality products such as fresh salmon, Scotch whisky, biscuits, jams and conserves, as well as beef and lamb carcasses and cheese.

Food From Britain is an organisation, funded by the Government and industry, which aims to assist the food and drink industry in Britain to improve its marketing at home and overseas. In Britain, it runs promotional campaigns and quality assurance schemes, among other marketing activities, and works with farmers and producers to develop market-led enterprises. Through its export association, the British Food Export Council, and its network of seven overseas offices, Food From Britain is able to identify market opportunities, provide introductions to buyers and arrange in-store promotions. Food From Britain also co-ordinates the British presence at major international food and drink trade exhibitions worldwide. The British Agricultural Export Committee of the London Chamber of Commerce represents exporters of technology, expertise and equipment. The Agricultural Engineers' Association represents exporters of agricultural and horticultural machinery. In 1991 Britain exported £2,080 million of farm machinery and spares.

One of the world's largest agricultural events, the annual Royal International Agricultural Exhibition, held at Stoneleigh in Warwickshire, provides an opportunity for visitors to see the latest techniques and improvements in British agriculture; over 189,000 visitors attended in 1992, of whom 25,500 were from overseas. Virtually every British agricultural machinery manufacturer is represented at the exhibition, which is also the most important pedigree livestock event in the country. Other major agricultural displays include the annual Royal Smithfield Show, held in London, which exhibits agricultural machinery, livestock and carcasses; the Royal Highland Show; the Royal Welsh Show; and the Royal Ulster Agricultural Show. There are also important regional shows.

Marketing

Agricultural products are marketed by private traders, producers' co-operatives and marketing boards. The latter are producers' organisations (each including a minority of independent members appointed by agriculture ministers) with certain statutory powers to regulate the marketing of milk, wool and potatoes. For the most part the boards buy from producers or control contracts between producers and first-hand buyers; the Potato Marketing Board, however, maintains only a broad control over marketing conditions, leaving producers free to deal individually with buyers. For home-grown cereals, meat and livestock, apples and pears, there are marketing organisations representing producer, distributor and independent interests.

The Milk Marketing Boards (one for England and Wales, three for Scotland and one for Northern Ireland), which legally have the right to purchase all unprocessed milk produced in

Britain, have announced plans to become voluntary co-operatives. Such a change would aim to make milk prices respond more to the demands of the market.

Food From Britain is responsible for improving the marketing of food and agricultural products, both in the domestic market and abroad. Its quality assurance schemes guarantee a repeatable quality in a number of product sectors.

Co-operatives

A substantial amount of agricultural and horticultural produce, such as grain, fruit and vegetables, is handled by marketing co-operatives, which had a turnover of £2,830 million in 1988. They have been formed to meet the demand from retailers for a continuous supply of fresh, quality produce. Food From Britain provides a range of advisory services for co-operatives.

Role of the Government

Four government departments have joint responsibility—the Ministry of Agriculture, Fisheries and Food; the Scottish Office Agriculture and Fisheries Department; the Welsh Office; and the Department of Agriculture for Northern Ireland.

Common Agricultural Policy

The European Community's Common Agricultural Policy (CAP) accounts for about two-thirds of the Community's budget. It aims to ensure stable agricultural markets and a fair standard of living for agricultural producers and to guarantee regular supplies of food at reasonable prices. For many commodities, annual minimum prices are set at which agencies of the member states will purchase products, and there are levies on imports to maintain internal support prices. Surpluses are bought by intervention boards (the Intervention Board executive agency in Britain) to be stored and sold when appropriate. Intervention stocks can be disposed of within the Community where this can be done without disrupting internal markets. Exports are facilitated by the provision of export refunds to bridge any gap between Community prices and world prices. In some cases, in particular in the beef and sheep sectors, there are also direct payments to producers—the suckler cow premium and the annual premium on ewes.

The support prices, as well as rates of levy, export refunds and other aids, are set in European Currency Units and are converted into the currencies of the member states at fixed rates of exchange—'green rates'—which can be out of line with the market rate of exchange between each currency and the European Currency Unit. Monetary compensatory amounts, based on the percentage difference between the green and market rates of each currency, are applied to prevent distortions in trade.

Nearly all the Community's agricultural expenditure (£24,105 million in 1991) is channelled through the European Agricultural Guidance and Guarantee Fund. The Fund's guarantee section finances market support arrangements, while the guidance section provides funds for structural reform—for example, farm modernisation and investment—and payments to assist certain farmers to change to alternative enterprises.

Agricultural production under the CAP has increased considerably in recent years, reflecting rapid technical progress and farming efficiency as well as the high level of price support. As consumption has remained relatively stable, this has resulted in the emergence of surpluses. Britain has consistently pressed for CAP reform, to bring supply and demand into better balance, to increase the role of market forces in agriculture and to make environmental considerations an integral part of the CAP. Since 1988 there has been a legally binding limit on CAP market support expenditure. Stabiliser mechanisms, brought in or extended for most CAP commodities, ensure that CAP support is automatically cut if production exceeds specified quantities. Significant price cuts of up to 20 per cent have already been made in a number of sectors.

Each annual price-fixing settlement since 1988 has consolidated this reform process, the cost being within the guidelines established by the Council of Ministers, and the stabiliser mechanisms have remained intact. The settlements have also helped to improve the competitive position of British farmers.

Reform

In 1991 the European Commission published detailed reform proposals for consideration by member states. Ministerial negotiations culminated in the agreement reached in May 1992 on measures to reform the CAP in the arable, milk, beef and sheepmeat sectors and on support prices for the 1992-93 marketing year.

Arable Crops

From the start of the 1993–94 marketing year, a new price support structure for cereals will come into effect. A new target price is to be established, and over three years this will be reduced progressively from the present level by about 30 per cent. An intervention price will set the minimum support level for Community cereals.

As a result of the price cuts, producers' returns for growing cereals are to be reduced. To compensate, producers will be offered a direct subsidy on an area basis provided that they agree to take 15 per cent of their arable land out of production. They will be required to do this from autumn 1992; those with only small arable areas, however, are exempt. If these measures prove less effective than expected in reducing production, the Community will be able to increase the 15 per cent level.

Pigs and Poultry

Pig and poultry farmers are expected to benefit from lower feed costs.

Beef

The intervention price for beef for 1992–93 has been frozen. From 1 July 1993 it will be reduced by 15 per cent over three years. Ceilings will be introduced progressively from the start of 1993 on the annual amount which may be purchased into intervention. This will be 750,000 tonnes in 1993, falling to 350,000 tonnes in 1997. In 1991–92 over 1 million tonnes of beef were purchased into intervention.

There will be a significant increase in the beef special premium (subject to regional ceilings on the number of claims) and the suckler cow premium paid to producers. There will be no headage limits on the suckler cow premium as originally proposed by the Community.

Sheep

Basic sheepmeat support prices for 1993 will remain at the 1992 level, but from 1993 ewe premium will be paid on individual producer quotas, which will set a limit on the number of animals eligible for ewe premium in future.

Milk

Milk support prices for 1992–93 have been frozen. In 1993–94 and 1994–95, however, the butter support price will be cut by 2.5 per cent a year. There will be no cuts in national milk production quotas for 1992–93. Quota cuts of 1 per cent in 1993–94 and 1994–95 have been agreed in principle, subject to Community review. Spain and Greece were granted additional milk quotas of 500,000 and 100,000 tonnes respectively with effect from April 1993.

Environment

All member states will run programmes to encourage environmentally sensitive farming. These schemes may be drawn from the following list:

—extensification[4] of crop or livestock production where this would be environmentally beneficial;

—organic farming;

—environmentally friendly management of farmland;

—environmental upkeep of abandoned land;

—setting aside farmland for at least 20 years for environmental purposes; and

—management of land for public access and recreation.

Member states have until June 1993 to draw up area programmes covering their entire territory.

Early Retirement

An early retirement scheme, designed to facilitate restructuring in those countries with large numbers of fragmented farms, will not be implemented in Britain where the average farm is already five times larger than in the Community as a whole.

Forestry

The agreement offers higher Community reimbursement for afforestation of agricultural land and for premium payments to farmers. It also offers limited premium payments to non-farmers, to aid the initial maintenance of trees.

GATT Uruguay Round

Agriculture was identified as a major issue for the Uruguay Round of the General Agreement on Tariffs and Trade launched in 1986.

---

[4]'Extensification' is the reduction of surpluses through the offer of financial payments to farmers to lessen production.

These negotiations aimed to achieve a freer and more market-oriented agricultural trading system and to agree cuts in production—and exemptions from them. The Community proposed reform on an aggregate measure of support, which would be reduced by 30 per cent between 1986 and 1996, with credit for reforms already made. Tariffs would replace other restrictions on market access, and be reduced over the next five years, with a corrective mechanism reflecting changes in world markets.

Negotiations resumed in 1991. Participants in the eighth round agreed to reach specific binding commitments on internal support, border measures and export competition.

Price Guarantees, Grants and Subsidies

Expenditure in Britain in 1991–92 on price guarantees, grants and subsidies and on CAP market regulations was estimated to be £350 million and £1,736 million respectively. About £1,745 million is to be reimbursed from the Community budget.

Potatoes and wool are not covered by the CAP; potato market support measures are operated through the Potato Marketing Board and the Department of Agriculture for Northern Ireland, and a price stabilisation fund for wool is administered by the British Wool Marketing Board. The Government intends to end the guarantee arrangements when parliamentary time permits.

Farmers are eligible for grants aimed at environmental enhancement of their farms and pollution control. Hill and upland farmers can also benefit from headage payments on cattle and sheep, known as compensatory allowances. Launching aid is available to production and marketing groups in the horticultural sector.

Public Expenditure under the CAP by the Intervention Board and the Agricultural Departments

FORECAST 1991/2

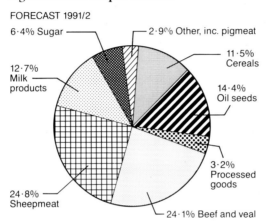

6·4% Sugar

2·9% Other, inc. pigmeat

12·7% Milk products

11·5% Cereals

14·4% Oil seeds

24·8% Sheepmeat

3·2% Processed goods

24·1% Beef and veal

In Less Favoured Areas (LFAs), where land quality is poor, farmers benefit from enhanced rates of grant and special payments on livestock. Their purpose is to support the continuation of livestock farming in the hill and upland areas, thereby conserving the countryside and maintaining a viable population in the LFAs.

Smallholdings and Crofts

Local authorities provide over 5,500 statutory smallholdings in England and just under 900 in Wales. They make loans of up to 75 per cent of required working capital to their tenants. Land settlement in Scotland has been carried out by the Government, which, while now seeking to dispose of holdings to its sitting tenants, still owns and maintains 120,228 hectares (296,963 acres) of land settlement estates, comprising 1,455 crofts and holdings.

In the crofting areas of Scotland (the former counties, in the Highlands and Islands, of Argyll, Inverness, Ross and Cromarty, Sutherland, Caithness, Orkney and Shetland) much of the land is held by tenants known as 'crofters'. They enjoy the statutory protection provided by crofting legislation and can benefit from government schemes which exist to support and help crofting communities. Most crofters are part-time or spare-time agriculturalists using croft income to supplement income from activities such as weaving, fishing, tourism and other occupations. The Crofters Commission has a statutory duty to promote the interests of crofters and to keep all crofting matters under review.

Tenancy Legislation

Approximately 35 per cent of agricultural land in England and Wales is tenanted. The agricultural holdings legislation protects the interests and rights of landlords and tenants, with provision for arbitration in the event of a dispute. Most agricultural tenants have the right to contest a notice to quit, which is then ineffective unless the landlord obtains consent to its operation from an independent body (in England and Wales, the Agricultural Land Tribunal and in Scotland, the Scottish Land Court). On termination of tenancy, the tenant is entitled to compensation in accordance with a special code. Under a practice known as 'conacre', occupiers in Northern Ireland not wishing to farm all their land let it annually to others. About one-fifth of agricultural land is let under this practice and is used mainly for grazing.

Agriculture and Protection of the Countryside

Agriculture ministers have a general duty, under the Agriculture Act 1986, to seek to achieve a reasonable balance between the needs of an efficient and stable agricultural industry and other interests in the countryside, including the conservation of its natural beauty and amenity and the promotion of its enjoyment by the public. In addition, they are required to further conservation of the countryside in the administration of farm capital grant schemes both in National Parks and in Sites of Special Scientific Interest designated by the nature conservancy bodies.

Environmentally Sensitive Areas

Under the Environmentally Sensitive Areas (ESA) Scheme, a British idea which other European Community members are following, 19 areas in Britain—ten in England, five in Scotland, two in Wales and two in Northern Ireland—have been designated. Twelve further areas in England, five in Scotland, four in Wales and two in Northern Ireland have been proposed for designation over the next couple of years. The Scheme is designed to help protect some of the most beautiful parts of the country from the damage and loss that can come from agricultural change. ESAs are notable for their landscape, wildlife or historic importance.

Since the Scheme began in 1987, each ESA's environmental and economic impact has been closely monitored. Following a review of the first areas, significant changes and improvements have been made to the Scheme, including opportunities for farmers to restore key environmental features of their land.

All the areas are unique and they are diverse in character. They include the heather moorlands of the North Peak and the

Agriculture and the Environment

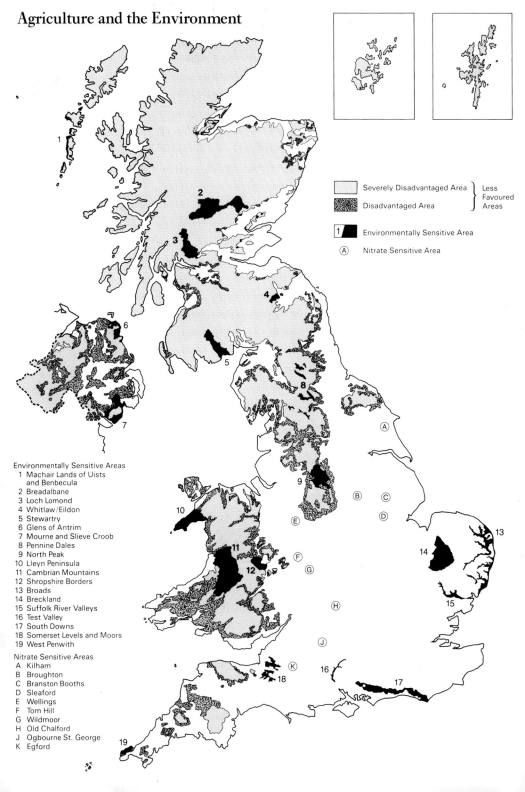

Severely Disadvantaged Area — Less Favoured Areas

Disadvantaged Area — Less Favoured Areas

1 Environmentally Sensitive Area

(A) Nitrate Sensitive Area

Environmentally Sensitive Areas
1 Machair Lands of Uists and Benbecula
2 Breadalbane
3 Loch Lomond
4 Whitlaw/Eildon
5 Stewartry
6 Glens of Antrim
7 Mourne and Slieve Croob
8 Pennine Dales
9 North Peak
10 Lleyn Peninsula
11 Cambrian Mountains
12 Shropshire Borders
13 Broads
14 Breckland
15 Suffolk River Valleys
16 Test Valley
17 South Downs
18 Somerset Levels and Moors
19 West Penwith

Nitrate Sensitive Areas
A Kilham
B Broughton
C Branston Booths
D Sleaford
E Wellings
F Tom Hill
G Wildmoor
H Old Chalford
J Ogbourne St. George
K Egford

Agricultural land use

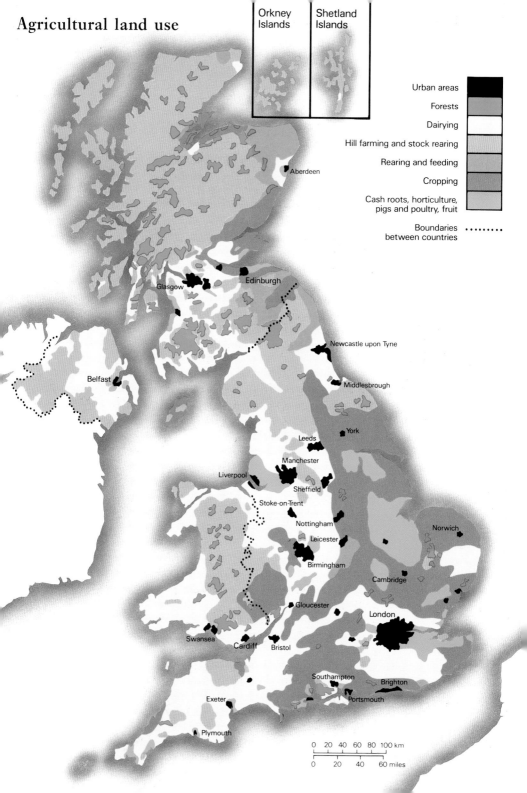

| Orkney Islands | Shetland Islands |

Urban areas
Forests
Dairying
Hill farming and stock rearing
Rearing and feeding
Cropping
Cash roots, horticulture, pigs and poultry, fruit
Boundaries between countries ·········

Aberdeen
Glasgow
Edinburgh
Newcastle upon Tyne
Belfast
Middlesbrough
York
Leeds
Manchester
Liverpool
Sheffield
Stoke-on-Trent
Nottingham
Norwich
Leicester
Birmingham
Cambridge
Gloucester
London
Swansea
Cardiff
Bristol
Southampton
Brighton
Portsmouth
Exeter
Plymouth

0 20 40 60 80 100 km

0 20 40 60 miles

Thomas Coke of Holkham, a famous innovator and encourager of good husbandry, inspecting his flock of Southdown sheep.

Right: ploughing in the Mynydd Eppynt (Powys), at Ty Capel near Llandewi Cwm, in July 1940, as part of the government wartime campaign to increase production.

Below: typical small farms in Northern Ireland between Crumlin and Lisburn in County Antrim.

Aberdeen Angus cows and calves—black polled beef cattle of high quality—at grass in eastern Scotland.

Right: Guernsey cows at a Buckinghamshire farm. This breed, famous for milk production, has been extensively exported since 1880.

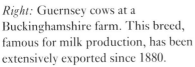

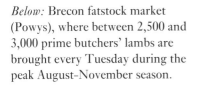

Below: Brecon fatstock market (Powys), where between 2,500 and 3,000 prime butchers' lambs are brought every Tuesday during the peak August-November season.

High-grade potato cultivation near Comber (County Down) in Northern Ireland.

Marsh Mill organic farm shop in Gloucestershire. Most organic farms have their own shops for direct selling to the public.

Growing field vegetables and bedding plants in peat blocks in glasshouses for transplanting by growers in the field is a speciality of Mill Farm at Harvington (Worcestershire).

Sheep in the Mourne and Slieve Croob ESA (see p.35) of Northern Ireland, where average farm size (17.4 hectares) is small even by Northern Ireland's standards.

Right: oilseed rape at Cookham Dean (Berkshire). More land was sown to oilseed rape in 1991, but output value declined by 5 per cent.

Hill farm, with the dry stone walls typical of northern areas—and Swaledale sheep—in the Lake District of northern England, classed as an LFA (see p.33).

Corn ricks at Lochbroom (Wester Ross). An unpolluted environment is in part a product of crofting practices.

Right: diversification—charcoal manufacture from coppiced deciduous woodland, a renewable energy source, on a Devon farm. Charcoal waste is compressed into briquettes, which are bagged and sold.

Below: view of the restocked areas of Beinn Lagan towards Glenbranter and Loch Eck in the Forestry Commission's Cowal district in mid-Scotland.

The old herring industry of Peterhead (Grampian), the most easterly town in Scotland, has given way to whitefish, which supply local processing plants.

Fish for sale to wholesalers at the dock in Grimsby, the largest fishing port in England, on the south side of the River Humber estuary.

A computer controlled system devised at AFRC's Silsoe Research Institute can weigh pigs without stress within a 5 per cent margin of accuracy, and monitor their behaviour and health.

New methods are being sought at the AFRC's Institute of Food Research to detect food poisoning organisms quickly and effectively.

grassland of the Broads in England; the landscape of the Cambrian Mountains in Wales; part of the coastal areas of the North and South Uists, Benbecula, Barra and Vatersay in the Outer Hebrides off north-west Scotland; and the steep sided glens and unique farming patterns of Antrim in Northern Ireland.

Participation in the ESA scheme is voluntary, and farmers enter into agreements with the relevant Ministry; initially these lasted for five years. In the reviewed areas ten-year agreements are offered—with a five-year break clause. An agreement specifies the agricultural management practices to be carried out by the farmer. Each ESA has varying tiers of management practices, from basic care and maintenance to more extensive forms of management. Details vary from one ESA to another, but all participants are prohibited from converting grassland to arable and are subject to restrictions on fertiliser and chemical usage. Most ESAs also restrict the numbers of stock that can be carried on the land as well as other operations—including the timing of cultivation. The annual payments are designed to compensate the farmers for reduced profitability, through the adoption of these less intensive production methods, and for the extra work that some management practices require. In Scotland additional payments are made for distinct items of conservation work set out in a mandatory farm conservation plan. Annual government expenditure on payments to farmers within ESAs throughout Britain is expected to rise to £64.5 million in 1994–95.

At the end of 1991 some 340,000 hectares (840,000 acres) of farmland were within the ESAs in England; 193,000 hectares (477,000 acres) in Wales; 220,000 hectares (540,000 acres) in Scotland; and 40,000 hectares (100,000 acres) in Northern Ireland. Some 3,100 farmers in England, 715 in Wales, 800 in Scotland and

1,030 in Northern Ireland have signed management agreements. Some 114,000 hectares (280,000 acres) in the English ESAs were covered by the agreements; 61,000 hectares (150,000 acres) in Wales; 120,000 hectares (300,000 acres) in Scotland; and 22,000 hectares (54,000 acres) in Northern Ireland.

Agricultural Buildings

The Government also intends to allow the extension to all areas of England and Wales of arrangements similar to those which apply in National Parks. These arrangements give local planning authorities discretion to examine and approve the siting, design and external appearance of new agricultural and forestry buildings. Authorities will also have to consider the desirability of preserving ancient monuments and their settings, known archaeological sites, the settings of listed buildings, and sites of recognised nature conservation. Full development control is to be extended to all farm holdings of less than 5 hectares (12 acres).

Other Schemes

Farmers are encouraged to develop new sources of income as an alternative to surplus production; this encouragement takes the form of grants to diversify into tourism and other non-agricultural activities on the farm. The Farm Woodland Premium Scheme, introduced in 1992, assists with the planting of woodlands on agricultural land, with incentives for broadleaved trees. Annual incentives of up to £250 a hectare are to be paid for either ten or 15 years, depending on the type of woodland created on arable or improved grassland. Annual incentives of £60 a hectare are to be paid for trees planted on unimproved grassland in the LFAs. Planting must not, in aggregate, exceed more than 50 per cent of any individual agricultural unit.

The European Community set-aside scheme, introduced in Britain in 1988, offers annual payments to farmers to take at least 20 per cent of their arable land out of agricultural production for five years. Additional payments for managing five-year set-aside land for the benefit of wildlife, landscape and the local community are available under the Countryside Premium Scheme (at present limited to eastern England). The Farm and Conservation Grant Scheme, part-funded by the European Community, provides grants for farmers to undertake environmental improvements and a limited range of farm investments. Under pilot Beef and Sheep Extensification Schemes, farmers receive annual compensation payments to reduce output by at least 20 per cent and to maintain this reduction over a five-year period. The Government has also designated ten nitrate-sensitive areas in England, where payments have been made to farmers who voluntarily undertake to restrict their agricultural practices and thus prevent unacceptable levels of nitrate leaching from farmland into water sources.

In 1991 the Government also published a Code of Good Agricultural Practice for the Protection of Water in England and Wales, which advises farmers on how best to avoid polluting watercourses. A pilot study is investigating whether pollution can be reduced by farmers drawing up their own waste disposal plans. Corresponding advice on water pollution in Scotland was published in 1992—a Code of Good Practice for the prevention of environmental pollution from agricultural activity.

In the Highlands and Islands of Scotland the Rural Enterprise Programme offers special funding, with Community support, to encourage farmers and crofters to develop new businesses.

Farm Diversification

Farm-based enterprises other than food production have become increasingly important. A survey published in 1991 calculated that diversified enterprises generated an average trading profit of over £5,000 a year, with 80 per cent of farmers considering their ventures to be successful. The most common diversification enterprises provide leisure activities such as golf courses, tourist accommodation, or riding. Often such enterprises are small-scale, with low financial returns. In contrast, many farmers run large-scale farm shops which make a substantial contribution to farm business income. Farm diversification is estimated to provide over 30,000 full-time jobs. The Government gives grants for some types of enterprise. At the end of June 1992 over £9 million had been committed.

Agricultural Training

The Agricultural Training Board receives government grant to arrange training for the agricultural industry. The Board has evolved a more strategic role, as a broker for training provision rather than as a direct course provider. A network of employer-led local boards has been set up to identify and arrange local training needs in co-operation with existing training providers (primarily agricultural colleges) and in liaison with Training and Enterprise Councils. Training provision is arranged through some 600 autonomous training groups throughout Great Britain. The Government proposes to change the Board's status so that it would become an independent non-statutory organisation and further develop commercially.

Professional, Scientific and Technical Services

In England and Wales the Agricultural Development and Advisory Service (ADAS), an executive agency, provides a wide range of professional, scientific and technical services for agriculture and its ancillary industries. Most types of advice and servicing are on a fee-paying basis, although initial advice to farmers on conservation, rural diversification (including use of land for woodlands) and animal welfare is available free. Similar services are provided in Scotland by the Scottish Office Agriculture and Fisheries Department through the Scottish Agricultural College. In Northern Ireland these services are available from the Department of Agriculture's agriculture and science services.

These organisations also advise the Government on the scientific, technical and business implications of policy proposals and assist in implementing policies concerning disease and pest eradication, food hygiene, animal welfare, land drainage and other capital grant schemes, and safeguarding agricultural land in relation to other land uses.

ADAS carries out research and development work under commission from the Ministry of Agriculture, Fisheries and Food, and works under contract directly for others and for levy-funded bodies. These undertakings are carried out at a range of experimental husbandry farms across England and Wales, and through regional centres or on clients' premises. The Central Science Laboratory also carries out research and development work commissioned by the Ministry.

Control of Diseases and Pests

Farm Animals

Britain is free from many serious animal illnesses. If they were to occur, diseases such as foot-and-mouth disease and classical swine fever would be combated by a slaughter policy applied to all animals infected or exposed to infection, and by control over animal movements during the outbreaks.

The Government has taken comprehensive measures to tackle the cattle disease bovine spongiform encephalopathy and to ensure that consumers are protected from any remote risk. It has:

—banned the feeding of ruminant protein to ruminants;

—ordered the destruction of the milk and carcasses of affected animals;

—banned from human or animal use those offals from other cattle which might be harbouring the agent; and

—committed significant funding for research.

It has also established an expert committee to advise on matters relating to spongiform encephalopathies.

The Government has ordered restrictions on the movement of pigs to prevent the spread of blue-eared pig disease.

Strict controls are exercised on the import of animals, birds, meat, and meat products so as to prevent the introduction of animal or avian diseases. Special measures apply to prevent the introduction of rabies, and dogs, cats and certain other mammals are subject to import licence and six months' quarantine. There are severe penalties for breaking the law. There have been no cases of rabies outside quarantine in Britain since 1970.

It is the responsibility of the livestock sector to dispose of its waste, including the carcasses of dead animals, within the framework of health and environmental restrictions. Research is in progress to find ways of minimising the cost of waste disposal. Professional advice and action on the control of animal disease and the welfare of farm livestock are the responsibility of the government State Veterinary Service. Its laboratory facilities and investigation centres perform specialist research work and advise private practitioners responsible for treating animals on the farm.

Fish

The fisheries departments operate statutory controls to prevent the introduction and spread of serious diseases of fish and shellfish. These controls include the licensing of live fish imports, the licensing of deposits of shellfish on the seabed, and movement restrictions on sites where outbreaks of notifiable diseases have been confirmed.

Plants

The agriculture departments are responsible for limiting the spread of plant pests and diseases and for preventing the introduction of new ones. They also issue the health certificates required by other countries to accompany plant material exported from Britain. Certification schemes encourage the development of healthy and true-to-type planting stocks.

Pesticides

There are strict controls on the supply and use of pesticides, and their maximum residue levels. All pesticides supplied in Britain must be approved for their safety and efficacy in use. Controls on pesticides are the joint responsibility of six government departments on the basis of advice from the independent Advisory Committee on Pesticides. The Government is currently reviewing pesticides approved before 1981.

Veterinary Medicinal Products

The manufacture, sale and supply of veterinary medicinal products are prohibited except under licence. Licences are issued by the agriculture ministers, who are advised on safety, quality and efficacy by the Veterinary Products Committee, which comprises independent experts.

Fisheries

Historical Background

Vast quantities of herring were caught in northern Europe in the Middle Ages. Beam trawls were used extensively in the North Sea and English Channel, particularly for flatfish. In the sixteenth century the English fished in the North Sea, off the Norwegian and Icelandic coasts, and as far as Newfoundland. In the late eighteenth century war with France and consequent lack of safety on the seas helped to stimulate the Scottish fisheries. By the early nineteenth century, however, the British were also fishing off Svalbard and off Greenland, and in the Gulf of St Lawrence. The nineteenth-century expansion in the fish trade owed much to better and quicker communications—Brixham (Devon) fishermen, for example, trawled from Dover and Ramsgate and supplied to the London market. By 1880 the British trawler fleet had over 1,000 vessels and in 1881 steam trawlers were introduced.

In the late 1940s Britain introduced factory trawlers, the catch being processed on board, an idea quickly developed by other countries. Overfishing and serious declines in stocks ensued. The need for controlled fishing, and the loss of fishing opportunities in distant waters, have resulted, since the early 1970s, in the reduction of Britain's distant-water trawler fleet, once numbering over 160 vessels (see below).

Policy and Potential

As one of the European Community's leading fishing nations, Britain plays an active role in the implementation and development of the Community's Common Fisheries Policy (CFP) agreed in 1983. The CFP covers access to coastal waters; the conservation and management of fish stocks; fisheries arrangements with third countries; the allocation of catch quotas among member states; the trade in and marketing of fish and fish products; and financial aid to promote the adaptation and development of the Community's fishing fleets.

Britain's fishing industry provides 59 per cent by quantity of British fish supplies, and is an important source of employment and income in a number of ports.

Cod, haddock, whiting, herring, plaice and sole are found in the North Sea off the east coasts of Scotland and England; mackerel, together with cod and other demersal fish, off the west coast of Scotland; sole, plaice, cod, herring and whiting in the Irish Sea; and mackerel, sole and plaice off the south-west coast of England. Nephrops, crabs, lobsters and other shellfish are found in the inshore waters all around the coast. At the end of 1990 there were 16,967 fishermen in regular employment and 5,088 occasionally employed. The Government aims to encourage the development of a viable, efficient and market-oriented fisheries industry within the CFP framework. Two main policy issues are conservation of fish stocks and capacity of the fleet.

Fish Caught

In 1990 demersal fish (caught on or near the bottom of the sea) accounted for 44 per cent by weight of total British landings; pelagic fish (caught near the surface) for 41 per cent and shellfish for 15 per cent. Landings of all types of fish (excluding salmon and trout) by British fishing vessels totalled 621,510 tonnes. Cod and haddock represented 23 and 18 per cent respectively of the total value of demersal and pelagic fish landed, while anglerfish (8 per cent), whiting (8 per cent), plaice (7 per cent), mackerel (5 per cent), and sole (4 per cent) were the other most important sources of earnings to the industry. The quayside value of the British catch of wetfish and shellfish in 1990 was £431 million and in the same year landings of nephrops represented 11 per cent of the total value of British landings of fish and shellfish.

Imports of fresh, frozen, cured and canned salt-water fish and shellfish in 1991 totalled 287,079 tonnes, those of freshwater fish 46,835 tonnes, those of fish meal 258,453 tonnes and those of fish oils 4,771 tonnes. Exports and re-exports of salt-water fish and fish products amounted to 390,267 tonnes, and those of freshwater fish to 23,622 tonnes.

The Fishing Fleet

At the end of 1991 the British fleet consisted of 10,871 registered vessels, including 424 deep-sea vessels longer than 24.4 m (80 ft). Among the main ports from which the fishing fleet operates are Aberdeen, Peterhead, Fraserburgh (Grampian); Lerwick (Shetland); Kinlochbervie, Ullapool (Highland); North Shields (Tyne and Wear); Grimsby (Humberside); Lowestoft (Suffolk); Brixham (Devon); Newlyn (Cornwall); and Kilkeel, Ardglass and Portavogie (Northern Ireland). With the extension of fishery limits to 200 miles, Britain's distant-water fleet was considerably reduced. A much smaller fleet has, however, continued to maintain its activities in distant waters.

The Government, in accordance with the CFP agreement, aims to conserve fish stocks, and to reduce total fish mortality, by restricting the time that fishing vessels may spend at sea, and to set down, as a licence condition, precisely how time at sea will be defined, notified and controlled. Its policy comprises decommissioning, an extension of licensing, technical conservation and 'effort control'. It is to make £25 million available for a cash-limited decommissioning scheme. Licensing is to be extended to the 7,000 vessels of 10 m and under in length.

Fish Farming

Fish farming production is centred on Atlantic salmon and rainbow trout, which are particularly suited to Britain's climate and waters. Production of salmon and trout has grown from less than 1,000 tonnes in the early 1970s to some 40,000 tonnes of salmon and 13,500 tonnes of trout in 1991. Scotland produces the largest amount of farmed salmon (40,000 tonnes in 1991—with a first-sale value of £130 million) in the European Community. Shellfish farming concentrates on molluscs such as oysters, mussels, clams and scallops, producing an estimated 5,000 tonnes a year.

The fish and shellfish farming industries make an important contribution to rural infrastructure, especially in remote areas such as the Highlands and Islands of Scotland. In 1991 these industries were estimated to have a combined wholesale turnover of some £150 million. Production is based on almost 1,200 businesses operating from some 1,800 sites and employing more than 5,000 people.

Administration

The fisheries departments are responsible for the administration of legislation concerning the fishing industry and for fisheries research. The safety and welfare of crews of fishing vessels and other matters common to shipping generally are provided for under legislation administered by the Department of Transport.

The Sea Fish Industry Authority is concerned with all aspects of the industry, including consumer interests. It undertakes research and development, provides training, and encourages quality awareness. It also administers a government grant scheme for fishing vessels, to promote a safe, efficient and modern fleet.

Fishery Limits

Only British vessels may fish within 6 miles of the coast; certain other Community member states have traditional fishing rights between 6 and 12 miles, as British vessels have in other member states' coastal waters. Outside 12 miles the only non-Community countries whose vessels may fish in Community waters are those with which the Community has reciprocal fisheries agreements (for example, Norway).

Common Fisheries Policy

The CFP's system for the conservation and management of the Community's fishing resources means that total allowable catches—with these decisions based partly on independent scientific advice—are set each year in order to conserve stocks. These catch levels are then allocated between member states on a fixed percentage basis, taking account of traditional fishing patterns. Activity is also regulated by a number of technical conservation measures, including minimum mesh sizes and the kind of gear used by fishermen, minimum landing sizes and closed areas designated mainly to protect young fish. Each member state is responsible for ensuring that its fishermen abide by the various fisheries' regulations and their performances are monitored by the Community's inspectors.

The 1983 settlement also covered the common organisation of the market in fish and fish products, and a policy for restructuring the Community fleet during 1987–97, designed to address the problem of over-capacity. The measures include financial assistance for the building and modernisation of fishing vessels.

Fishery relations between the European Community and other countries are extensive and are governed by different agreements. Those of most importance to Britain are with Norway, Greenland, the Faroe Islands and Sweden. Annual Community quotas have also been established in international waters in the north-west Atlantic and around Svalbard.

Fish Hygiene Directive

The single European market aims to facilitate trade among Community members and to protect public health by harmonising measures for the handling and treatment of all fish and shellfish (including aquaculture products) at all stages up to, but excluding, retail level. It will take effect from 1 January 1993, and lays down rules to ensure the safe and hygienic handling of fish and fish products. This includes the conditions on board factory vessels; requirements during and after landing, including auction markets on shore; and establishments on land, primarily processors. The single market provisions also lay down the conditions for processed products, as well as hygiene rules for those who come into contact with fish and fish products.

Salmon and Freshwater Fisheries

Salmon and sea-trout are fished commercially in inshore waters around the British coast. Eels and elvers are also taken commercially both in estuaries and in freshwater. Angling for salmon and sea-trout (game fishing) and for other freshwater species (coarse fishing) is popular throughout Britain. In England and Wales fishing is licensed by the National Rivers Authority; in Scotland salmon fishing is administered by Salmon District Fishery Boards. In Northern Ireland fishing is licensed by the Fisheries Conservancy Board for Northern Ireland and the Foyle Fisheries Commission in their respective areas, and 65 public angling waters, including salmon, trout and coarse fisheries, are accessible to Department of Agriculture permit holders.

Agriculture, Fisheries and Food Research

The total government-funded programme of research and development in agriculture, fisheries and food in 1992–93 amounts to some £305 million, including funding by the Ministry of Agriculture, Fisheries and Food, the Scottish Office Agriculture and Fisheries Department, the Department of Agriculture for Northern Ireland and from the Office of Science and Technology budget. The agriculture departments, the Agricultural and Food Research Council (AFRC) and private industry share responsibility for research, which is carried out in a network of research institutes, specialist laboratories and experimental husbandry farms; with Horticulture Research International (HRI; established in 1990); and in higher education institutions.

Agriculture and Food Research

The research aims to maintain an efficient and competitive industry in Britain consistent with high standards of animal welfare and care for the environment. The work of the AFRC and the agriculture departments is co-ordinated into national programmes, primarily on the recommendations of the Priorities Board for Research and Development in Agriculture and Food. The Board advises on the research needs and on the allocation of available resources between and within areas of research.

Among the AFRC's main research areas are plant science, arable crops, horticulture, grassland and environmental research, animal physiology and genetics, food research, and agricultural engineering. Funding for 1992–93 will enable further work to be done in intracellular signalling (the chemical language by which cells within plants and animals communicate); global environmental research; plant molecular biology; and stem cell biology. Recent developments include the completion of the Transgenic Animals Programme, which extends existing transgenic work in mice to farm livestock and the genetic manipulation of proteins in the animals' milk. Significant advances have been made in the study of plant reproductive processes and plant/herbivore interactions. New programmes have been launched, including a study of the transport of pollutants in soils and rocks, and a working group has been set up to examine the use of animals in research.

The AFRC, a non-departmental public body, receives funds (£139.3 million in 1991–92) from the science budget through the Office of Science and Technology, and has income from work commissioned by the Ministry of Agriculture, Fisheries and Food, by industry and by other bodies. The Council is responsible for research carried out in its seven institutes and in British higher education institutions, through its research grants scheme. In addition to commissioning research with the AFRC and other organisations, such as HRI, the Ministry commissions research and development at its Food Science Laboratory, at the Central Veterinary Laboratory, at the Central Science Laboratory, and with ADAS.

The five Scottish Agricultural Research Institutes, funded by the Scottish Office Agriculture and Fisheries Department, cover areas of research complementary to those of the AFRC institutes, while including work relevant to the soils, crops and livestock of northern Britain. Development work in Scotland is carried out by the Scottish Agricultural College, which operates from three centres.

In Northern Ireland basic, strategic and applied research is carried out by the Department of Agriculture in its specialist research divisions and at its three agricultural colleges. It also has links with the Queen's University of Belfast and the Agricultural Research Institute of Northern Ireland.

Agricultural research is also conducted or sponsored by private industry, in particular by related industries such as agrochemicals and agricultural machinery.

In addition, the food industry funds or undertakes relevant research. The Government funds strategic research essential for the public good, for example, into food safety, human health, animal welfare and flood protection, but has withdrawn funding from research which promises commercial application or exploitation within a reasonable timescale—for which it looks to industry to take on a greater degree of funding.

In 1992–93 the Ministry will spend £30 million of its £131 million annual research budget on research relevant to the environment. This includes the protection of the countryside, water supplies and rivers; ensuring that straw and other crop residues are disposed of other than by burning—a practice to be banned after the 1992 harvest; reducing the use of pesticides to the minimum compatible with efficient production; flood and coastal defences; and care of the marine environment. By the end of 1992–93 the Ministry will have spent £12 million on research into bovine spongiform encephalopathy.

Fisheries and Aquatic Environment Research

The Ministry of Agriculture, Fisheries and Food laboratories deal with marine and freshwater fisheries, shellfish, marine pollution, fish farming and disease. Research work is also commissioned by the Ministry with the Natural Environment Research Council, with the Sea Fish Industry Authority and with a number of universities. The Ministry has two seagoing research vessels. In Scotland, the Scottish Office Agriculture and Fisheries Department undertakes a similar, and complementary, range of research and also has two seagoing vessels. The Department of Agriculture laboratories in Northern Ireland undertake research on marine and freshwater fisheries, and also have a seagoing research vessel.

Forestry

Until about 2500 BC Great Britain was almost entirely covered by trees. In Scotland, the extensive forest of Caledon, known to the Romans in the third century AD, seems to have occupied the most fertile lowlands and valleys throughout the central Highlands. By the end of the seventeenth century the woodland area of Great Britain had diminished to about 12 per cent and by the late nineteenth century it had fallen to about 5 per cent of the land surface—a smaller proportion than almost any other country in Europe.

Woodland now covers an estimated 2.35 million hectares (5.8 million acres) in Britain: about 7 per cent of England, 15 per cent of Scotland, 12 per cent of Wales and 6 per cent of Northern Ireland—about 10 per cent of the total land area and well below the 25 per cent average for the whole of Europe. The Government supports the continued expansion of forestry which makes an increasing contribution to meeting the national demand for timber; brings employment in forestry and related industries; creates opportunities for recreation and public access to the countryside; is a component of landscapes and a habitat for wildlife; and provides an effective means by which carbon dioxide can be absorbed from the atmosphere and stored over long periods. Over 230,000 hectares (570,000 acres) of new forest have been created during the last decade, mainly on the initiative and enterprise of private owners.

The area of productive forest in Great Britain is 2.15 million hectares (5.3 million acres), 40 per cent of which is managed by the Forestry Commission. The rate of new planting in 1991–92 was 2,999 hectares (7,410 acres) by the Commission and 14,270 hectares (35,260 acres) by other woodland owners, with the help of grants from the Commission, mainly in Scotland. The planting of broadleaved trees is encouraged on suitable sites and in 1991–92, 7,070 hectares (17,470 acres) of broadleaved trees were planted. An increasing proportion of new planting is by private owners.

The Commission's expanded Woodland Grant Scheme pays establishment grants to help in the creation of new woodlands and forests and for the regeneration of existing ones. It highlights such features as native tree species, woody shrubs, short-rotation coppice and agroforestry. Management grants under the scheme contribute to the cost of managing woodlands to provide silvicultural, environmental and social benefits. Supplements are available for planting community woodlands and for planting on better land.

Total employment in state and private forests in Great Britain was estimated at 42,000 in 1990, including about 10,000 people engaged in the haulage and processing of home-grown timber.

Wood production has nearly doubled since 1970. British woodlands meet 15 per cent of the nation's consumption of wood and wood products. The volume of timber harvested on Commission lands in 1991–92 totalled 3.9 million cubic metres (137 million cubic feet).

Species of Tree in Great Britain

Native Trees

Nearly 1,700 types of tree, several hundred of which are common in the landscape, can be found in Britain, with some 33 species native to Great Britain. Oak, of two main types, is the most common English tree and is resistant to wind; large areas were planted with oak in the past for timber for shipbuilding and for the iron industry.

Other species include the wych elm; lime, still common as a forest tree in some ancient woods such as Sherwood Forest (Nottinghamshire); ash, once valued for its strength; and beech, a good shade bearer with timber versatile for indoor uses. Yew, a very hard wood, is one of the three native British conifers, the others being Scots pine and juniper, the most ancient native British tree. Silver birch is found throughout England, Wales and Scotland, and is renowned for its hardiness, being able to withstand extremes of temperature. Scots pine, widespread in Great Britain in prehistoric times and producing good general purpose timber, is now native only to Scotland, although it has been reintroduced throughout England and Wales.

Trees for Timber
Norway spruce (the Christmas tree), introduced from Europe from the mid-sixteenth century, produces a high volume of general purpose timber. Other species introduced for planting, mainly from the nineteenth century, include Sitka spruce, now planted more widely in Britain than any other tree and giving first-class pulpwood; European and Japanese larch; Corsican pine; and lodgepole pine, a good pioneer species. Douglas fir grows to a great height, as do two other types of fir, grand and noble, planted throughout Great Britain. Southern beech, planted from the 1960s, grows as fast as most conifers but tends not to flourish in the colder parts of the country.

The number of broadleaved native trees capable of producing timber for industry is small, and compared with many conifer species their yields are low. The average yield of all broadleaves in Great Britain is about 5 cubic metres (178 cubic feet) per hectare a year, while that for conifers is about 11 cubic metres (388 cubic feet). Of the native conifers, only the Scots pine is an important timber tree, averaging about 9 cubic metres per hectare a year.

The Forestry Commission and Forestry Policy

The Forestry Commission, established in 1919, is the national forestry authority in Great Britain. The Commissioners give advice on forestry matters and are responsible to the Secretary of State for Scotland, the Minister of Agriculture, Fisheries and Food, and the Secretary of State for Wales.

Within the Commission, reorganised in 1992, the Forestry Authority administers felling licence procedures; provides advice to private woodland owners; administers payment of grants for approved planting and restocking schemes; and liaises with local authorities and woodland and countryside groups. Forest Enterprise develops and manages the Commission's forests and forestry estate as a multiple-use resource, providing timber for the wood-using industries and opportunities for recreation, and it is responsible for nature conservation and the forest environment. A Policy and Resources Group is responsible for parliamentary business, policy development, and European and international liaison.

The Commission has sold 79,000 hectares (195,000 acres) of plantation and plantable land since 1981 and has been asked by the Government to dispose of a further 100,000 hectares (247,000 acres) by the end of the century. The Commission is financed partly by the Government and partly by receipts from sales of timber and other produce, and from rents.

Forestry Initiatives

The Forestry Commission and the Countryside Commission plan to create 12 community forests (covering between 10,000 and

20,000 hectares each—40 to 80 sq miles) on the outskirts of major cities in England. These include the Great North Forest (Tyne and Wear), the Forest of Mercia (Staffordshire) and Thames Chase, east of London. As part of its rural initiative for Wales, the Government plans to give local communities greater involvement in the development of 35,000 hectares (135 sq miles) of forest in the coalfield valleys of South Wales—about 20 per cent of the land area—owned by the Forestry Commission. A Central Scotland Woodland Initiative has also been launched; more than 6 million trees have been planted.

Farm Woodland Scheme: Trees Approved for Planting 1 October 1988 to 30 September 1991

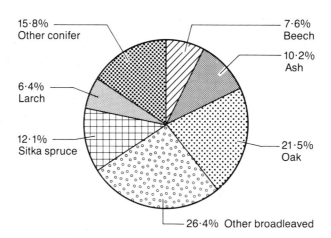

15·8% Other conifer
7·6% Beech
10·2% Ash
6·4% Larch
12·1% Sitka spruce
21·5% Oak
26·4% Other broadleaved

Total broadleaved approved for planting – 12,781,000
Total conifer approved for planting – 6,696,907
Total all species approved for planting – 19,477,907

Forestry Research

The Forestry Authority maintains two principal research stations, at Alice Holt Lodge near Farnham (Surrey) and at Bush Estate near Edinburgh, for basic and applied research into all aspects of forestry. Aid is also given for research work in universities and other institutions. A database on forestry and tree-related research in Great Britain has been compiled by the Forestry Research Co-ordination Committee and is updated annually.

The Forestry Authority conducts an annual forest health survey which monitors the effects of air pollution and other stress factors on a range of broadleaves and conifers. It has increased research into wildlife conservation and farm forestry, including an evaluation of agroforestry systems combining wide-spaced conifers and broadleaves with sheep grazing. The Government has set up an expert scientific review group to advise on tree health in Britain.

Forestry in Northern Ireland

The Department of Agriculture may acquire land for afforestation and give financial and technical assistance for private planting. The state forest area has grown steadily since 1945. By 1992, 75,000 hectares (185,000 acres) of plantable land had been acquired, of which 60,000 hectares (148,250 acres) were planted. There were 16,000 hectares (39,500 acres) of privately owned forest. Some 500 professional and industrial staff work in state forests. There are nine forest parks.

In the eighteenth and nineteenth centuries the sycamore, beech and horse chestnut, and softwoods such as silver and spruce fir and Scots pine, were introduced. Sitka spruce and lodgepole pine were first planted in the nineteenth century. State planting began in 1903.

Addresses

Agricultural Development and Advisory Service, Ergon House, 17 Smith Square, London SW1P 3HX.

Agricultural and Food Research Council, Polaris House, North Star Avenue, Swindon SN2 1UH.

Agricultural Training Board, 59 London Road, Horsham, West Sussex RH12 1AN.

British Agricultural Export Council, 69 Cannon Street, London EC4N 5AB.

Food From Britain, 301–344 Market Towers, 1 Nine Elms Lane, London SW8 5NQ.

Forestry Commission, 231 Corstorphine Road, Edinburgh EH12 7AT.

Institute for Animal Health, Compton, Newbury, Berkshire RG16 0NN.

Intervention Board, Fountain House, 2 Queen's Walk, Reading, Berkshire RG1 7QW.

Ministry of Agriculture, Fisheries and Food, 3 Whitehall Place, London SW1A 2HH.

Department of Agriculture for Northern Ireland, Dundonald House, Upper Newtownards Road, Belfast BT4 3SB.

Scottish Office Agriculture and Fisheries Department, Pentland House, 47 Robb's Loan, Edinburgh EH14 1TW.

Welsh Office, Cathays Park, Cardiff CF1 3NQ.

Further Reading

£

Advisory Services to Agriculture.
National Audit Office.
ISBN 0 10 235891 5.   HMSO   1991   6.70

Animals in Transit. Third Report of the House
of Commons Agriculture Committee, Session
1990–91.
Vol. 1. Report and Proceedings of the
Committee.
ISBN 0 10 287791 2.   HMSO   1991   6.40
Vol. 2. Memoranda, Minutes of Evidence and
Appendices.
ISBN 0 10 287891 2.   HMSO   1991   22.00

Animals in Transit: Third Special Report.
Government Response to the Third Report
from the House of Commons Agriculture
Committee, Session 1990–91.
ISBN 0 10 267891 X.   HMSO   1991   1.90

Balance in the Countryside.   MAFF Publications   1991

SIMON BELL
Community Woodland Design: Guidelines.
Forestry Commission.
ISBN 0 11 710300 4.   HMSO   1992   9.75

Bovine Spongiform Encephalopathy.
Government Response to the Fifth Report
from the House of Commons Agriculture
Committee, Session 1989–90.
ISBN 0 10 113282 4.   HMSO   1991   2.90

Commodity Markets in the 1990s: Cereals. First
Report from the House of Commons
Agriculture Committee, Session 1991–92.
Vol. 1. Report and Proceedings of the
Committee.
ISBN 0 10 271292 1.   HMSO   1992   7.15
Vol. 2. Minutes of Evidence and Appendices.
ISBN 0 10 117782 8.   HMSO   1992   22.00

Commodity Markets in the 1990s: Cereals.
Government Response to the First Report
from the House of Commons Agriculture
Committee, Session 1991–92.
ISBN 0 10 227892 X.   HMSO   1992   1.45

IAN CUNNINGHAM
Forestry Expansion: A Study of Technical,
Economic and Ecological Factors.   Forestry Commission   1991

Development and Future of the Common
Agricultural Policy. Sixteenth Report from the
House of Lords Committee on the European
Communities, Session 1990–91.
Vol. 2. Evidence.
ISBN 0 10 485791 9.   HMSO   1991   26.00

Food Advisory Committee Report on its Review
of Food Labelling and Advertising 1990.
ISBN 0 11 242913 0.   HMSO   1991   11.25

SUSAN FOREMAN
Loaves and Fishes: an Illustrated History of the
Ministry of Agriculture, Fisheries and Food,
1889–1989.
Ministry of Agriculture, Fisheries and Food.
ISBN 0 11 242823 1.   HMSO   1989   7.95

Forestry Policy for Great Britain.   Forestry Commission   1991

B.G. HIBBERD (editor)
Farm Woodland Practice. Forestry Commission
Handbook 3.
ISBN 0 11 710265 2.   HMSO   1988   7.50

B.G. HIBBERD (editor)
Urban Forestry Practice. Forestry Commission
Handbook 5.
ISBN 0 11 710273 3.   HMSO   1989   11.50

S.J. HODGE
Urban Trees: A Survey of Street Trees in
England.
Forestry Commission Bulletin 99.
ISBN 0 11 710299 7.   HMSO   1991   3.50

J.L. INNES and R.C. BOSWELL
Monitoring of Forest Condition in Great Britain
1990.
Forestry Commission Bulletin 98.
ISBN 0 11 710298 9.   HMSO   1991   7.50

JOHN McINERNEY and MARTIN TURNER
Patterns, Performance and Prospects in Farm
Diversification.   University of Exeter   1991   7.50

MINIM 1990—A Guide to MAFF's Work
1989-1994.   MAFF Publications   1991   21.50

Monitoring our Food and Nutrition.
Food Safety Directorate, Ministry of
Agriculture, Fisheries and Food.   Food Sense   1992

Our Farming Future.   MAFF Publications   1991

*Permitted Development Rights for Agriculture
and Forestry.*
Department of the Environment Planning
Research Programme.
ISBN 0 11 752414 X.   HMSO   1991   7.70

*Pesticide Poisoning of Animals 1991:
Investigations of Suspect Incidents of Great
Britain.*   MAFF Publications   1992   2.95

*Pesticides 1992: Pesticides approved under the
Control of Pesticides Regulations.*
Ministry of Agriculture, Fisheries and Food
and Health and Safety Executive.
ISBN 0 11 242924 6.   HMSO   1992   13.50

*Report on the Effects of the Milk Marketing
Scheme 1933 on Consumers.*   MAFF Publications   1991   2.95

*Report on Wages in Agriculture: 1 January to
31 December 1990.*
Ministry of Agriculture, Fisheries and Food.
ISBN 0 11 242920 3.   HMSO   1991   3.50

*Safer Food: Local Authorities and the Food
Safety Act 1990.*
Department of Health and Ministry of
Agriculture, Fisheries and Food.
ISBN 0 11 242897 5.   HMSO   1990   19.75

The Trade Gap in Food and Drink. Second
Report from the House of Commons
Agriculture Committee, Session 1991–92.
Vol. 1. Report and Proceedings of the
Committee.
ISBN 0 10 288792 6.   HMSO   1992   6.20
Vol. 2. Minutes of Evidence and Appendices.
ISBN 0 10 289192 3.   HMSO   1992   32.50

The Trade Gap in Food and Drink.
Government Reply to the Second Report of
the Agriculture Committee, Session 1991–92.
Ministry of Agriculture, Fisheries and Food.
ISBN 0 10 119822 1.   HMSO   1992   1.95

Annual Reports and Statistics

Advisory Committee on Novel Foods and Processes

Department of Health

Advisory Committee on Pesticides		HMSO
Agriculture in Scotland.		
Scottish Office Agriculture and Fisheries Department		HMSO
Agriculture in the United Kingdom	MAFF	HMSO
Central Veterinary Laboratory		MAFF
Crofters Commission		HMSO
Digest of Environmental Protection and Water Statistics.		
Department of the Environment		HMSO
Expert Group on Animal Feedingstuffs		HMSO
Farm Incomes in the United Kingdom	MAFF	HMSO
Food From Britain		FFB
Forestry Commission		HMSO

Household Food Consumption and Expenditure.
National Food Survey Committee   HMSO

Office of Water Services   HMSO

Report of Forest Research.
Forestry Commission   HMSO

Veterinary Medicines Directorate   VMD

Index

Printed in the UK for **HMSO**.
Dd 0294548, 12/92, C30, 51-2423, **5673**.

A MONTHLY UPDATE

CURRENT AFFAIRS:
A MONTHLY SURVEY

Using the latest authoritative information from official and other sources, *Current Affairs* is an invaluable digest of important developments in all areas of British affairs. Focusing on policy initiatives and other topical issues, its factual approach makes it the ideal companion for *Britain Handbook* and *Aspects of Britain*. Separate sections deal with governmental; international; economic; and social, cultural and environmental affairs. A further section provides details of recent documentary sources for these areas. There is also a twice-yearly index.

Annual subscription including index and postage £35·80 net. Binder £4·95.

Buyers of Britain 1993: An Official Handbook qualify for a discount of 25 per cent on a year's subscription to Current Affairs (see next page).

HMSO Publications Centre
(Mail and telephone orders only)
PO Box 276
LONDON SW8 5DT
Telephone orders: 071 873 9090

THE ANNUAL PICTURE

BRITAIN HANDBOOK

The annual picture of Britain is provided by *Britain: An Official Handbook* - the forty-fourth edition will be published early in 1993. It is the unrivalled reference book about Britain, packed with information and statistics on every facet of British life.

With a circulation of over 20,000 worldwide, it is essential for libraries, educational institutions, business organisations and individuals needing easy access to reliable and up-to-date information, and is supported in this role by its sister publication, *Current Affairs: A Monthly Survey*.

Approx. 500 pages; 24 pages of colour illustrations; 16 maps; diagrams and tables throughout the text; and a statistical section. Price £19·50.

Buyers of Britain 1993: An Official Handbook *have the opportunity of a year's subscription to* Current Affairs *at 25 per cent off the published price of £35·80. They will also have the option of renewing their subscription next year at the same discount. Details in each copy of* Handbook, *from HMSO Publications Centre and at HMSO bookshops (see back of title page).*